red rhino
b**OO**k s®
NONFICTION

SADDLEBACK
EDUCATIONAL PUBLISHING
www.sdlback.com

ISBN-13: 978-1-68021-032-3
ISBN-10: 1-68021-032-7
eBook: 978-1-63078-339-6

Printed in Singapore by Craft Print International Ltd
0000/CA00000000

19 18 17 16 15   1 2 3 4 5

TABLE OF
CONTENTS

Chapter 1

MAY DAY FESTIVAL

It is a bright spring day.

The river flows.

Birds sing.

Then they go quiet.

People are coming.

Who are they?

They put up a pole.

Long ribbons hang from it.

Then the people form a circle.

They begin to sing.

A drum thumps.

The singing stops.

Each person takes a ribbon.

Some move right.

Others move left.

Thump. Thump. Thump.

Faster and faster.

People *weave* the ribbons.

In and out.

In and out.

The pole is covered.

Then everyone stands still.
A woman comes forward.
She says some words.
She touches the pole.
She asks for good luck.
Another comes forward.
He asks for a *blessing*.

What is going on?
Who are these people?
They are witches.
But few people know it.

Chapter 2
ARE WITCHES REAL?

Witch.

It is just a word.

It may sound scary.

You may think of a woman.

She is old.

She rides a broomstick.

She laughs.

She does bad magic.

Where did this idea come from?

It was long ago.

There were few doctors.

But there were wise women.

And a few men.

WITCH WISDOM

Where does the word "witch" come from? Nobody knows.

They knew about plants.
They made medicine.
A drink for a fever.
A lotion for a burn.
A bandage for a sprain.

People trusted them.

They knew everyone.

They kept secrets.

Some did not like this.

The Roman Catholic Church.

The Church wanted people's trust.

And *loyalty*.

They said witches were bad.

People got scared.

Witches were jailed.

Many were killed.

So they hid.

Worked in secret.

There were trials.
They started in Europe.
Then they came to America.
To *colonial* Hartford. Then Salem.
There were laws.
No witches. No magic.
It was a crime.

There is still fear today.

Most witches stay hidden.

They keep quiet. Work alone.

They may trust other witches.

And form a group.

They call it a *coven*.

Chapter 3
WHAT IS A WITCH?

Is magic real? Or is it just tricks?

Witches believe it is real.

Magic is powerful.

A force of nature.

It joins people.

To the earth. To each other.

And to all living things.

Witches do magic.

They say words.

They move their hands.

Some make spells.

Some tell *fortunes*.

Others talk to ghosts.

Some witches have no religion.

Others are *pagan*.

They believe in many gods.

They love the earth.

Wicca is pagan.

Wiccan witches obey one law.
It says harm none.
They trust in *karma*.
It is about balance.
Bad acts are punished.
Good acts are rewarded.

There are other kinds of witches.
A green witch loves nature.
This witch likes to grow plants.
A hedge witch helps the sick.
This witch can talk to ghosts.
A kitchen witch does magic
in the kitchen.
This witch is a great cook.

Most witches have jobs.
And families.
They like some things.
And not others.
That's why there are so many
different kinds.

WITCH WISDOM

A male witch is called a witch. Not a warlock.

Chapter 4
MAGICAL TOOLS

A magic wand.

A broom.

An iron pot.

These are tools.

Some witches use them.

Others do not.

It depends.

There are no rules.

Tools help with *focus*.

They calm the mind.

Tools move energy.

Energy is everywhere.

In the air we breathe.

And in the ground we walk on.

There is a long stick.

It is made of wood.

Usually ash.

It has a forked top.

It's called a stang.

Use it as a walking stick.

Or as a wand.

Poke it in the ground.

Then it's an *altar*.

WITCH WISDOM

A witch bottle is a magical tool. It protects people from bad magic. A bottle from 1748 was found in Essington, PA, in 1976.

Most wands are shorter.

They can be wood.

Metal.

Or even *crystal*.

There are brooms.

They are called besoms.

They sweep out bad energy.

But they don't touch the floor.

They are stored upright.

Bristles up.

Why?

To keep in the good luck.

Pots are used to make potions.

A *cauldron* is a pot.

It is made of iron.

Many have three legs.

There are other tools.

Like bones.

Wishbones are charms.

Charms have magic power.

Have you ever pulled a wishbone?

Did it bring you luck?

That idea came from a witch.

Chapter 5
MAGIC SPELLS

Spells are words. Spoken or silent.

These words have magic power.

There are safety spells.

Get well spells.

Money spells. Love spells.

You have to believe in magic.

Or a spell will not work.

There are some rules. Steps to follow.

What steps? First have a goal.

Think about what you want.

Maybe it's luck. Maybe it's money.

Just keep it simple.

WITCH WISDOM

A *grimoire* is a book of magic spells. The oldest were written on clay. They are from the ancient city of Uruk.

Then check the timing.
It depends on the spell.
Time of day?
Winter or summer? Spring or fall?
Full moon? Or no moon?
Some times are more powerful.
And the extra energy helps.

Next get supplies.

But only if they are needed.

Maybe it's a plant.

A crystal. Or a candle.

Fix the space. Prepare the supplies.

Use a tool. Say the spell.

Believe it will happen.

Is it that easy? No!

Magic is work. It takes practice.

Chapter 6

HEXES AND CURSES

A *hex* is a spell.

It has bad energy.

It brings bad luck to a person.

But it does not last long.

A *curse* is a spell too.

It is the worst kind of magic.

Black magic.

It can hurt people.

Make them sick.

Or even kill them.

Things can be cursed.
Like the Hope Diamond.
It was in a statue.
Then it was stolen.
It brought bad luck.
Illness. And even death.
It killed kings. And ruined families.
Was it really magic? Or chance?

A pharaoh's tomb was cursed.
To guard its treasure.
Keep it safe.
Many who found it died.
Or so it was said.

Hexes and curses can be broken.

There are many ways.

Spells. Magical dolls.

Even mirrors.

They make bad energy bounce back.

So watch out!

WITCH WISDOM

The Hope Diamond is big. It is the same size as a walnut. It is 45.5 carats. And worth $250 million.

Chapter 7

AMAZING PLANTS

Eye of *newt*?

Toe of frog?

What's that?

It's code.

For mustard seed.

And buttercup.

Why use code?

So others don't know.

Witches have their own recipes.

They keep them secret.

Witches use many plants.

Some are herbs.

They can cure us.

Make us well.

Just like drugs.

Need first aid?

Plants can help.

Aloe for small burns.

Yarrow for cuts.

Ginger for tummy aches.

The easiest cure?

Herbal tea!

Can a plant change your luck?

Witches think so.

Mint brings money.

Poppies bring good luck.

Sage brings wisdom.

Plants also have power.

Add them to a spell.

Add them to a potion.

Wham! It's stronger.

But beware!

Some are dangerous.

Witches use plants at home.

They crush bay leaves.

Put them by the door.

Why? To stop bad magic.

They sprinkle garlic powder too.

Why? To keep ghosts out.

Chapter 8
THE SPIRIT WORLD

Do you believe in ghosts? Many do.
Some witches say they
can talk to ghosts.
How? There are many ways.
Some use tools.
Like a crystal ball.
Or a spirit board.

Most crystal balls are *quartz*.
Quartz is a *mineral*.
Crystal is *reflective*.
A witch gazes into it.
Their mind goes blank.
Their vision blurs.

Then they see things.

The past.

And the future.

Clouds appear.

White ones are good.

Black ones are bad.

Be careful!

The crystal is like a door.

Good spirits can see it.

But so can bad ones.

There is another way to talk to the dead.

With a spirit board.

It is called a Ouija board.

The board has printed letters.

Numbers. And other signs.

There is another piece.

A smaller board.

It is shaped like a heart.

How does the board work?

Here is an example.

It is night.

The room is quiet.

Someone leads a group.

Usually a witch.

They sit around a table.

The Ouija board is in the middle.

Everyone can reach it.

Fingertips are on the smaller board.

Questions are asked.

A spirit comes.

Answers are spelled out.

Chapter 9

TELLING FORTUNES

Some witches like telling fortunes.

They guess the future.

This is a *psychic* gift.

But how is it done?

Reading cards is one way.

The cards are called tarot.

Palm reading is another.

Tarot was a game.

It started long ago.

A deck has 78 cards.

Each has a picture.

The cards are chosen.

They tell a story.

Your story.

Palm reading is older.

It began in ancient India.

Around 500 BC.

Palms have lines.

There are three main ones.

Heart. Or feelings.

Head. Or the mind.

Life. Or happiness.

The right hand is the future.

And the outer self.

The left hand is the past.

And the inner self.

43

Reading cards.
Studying palms.
Is it magic?
Many think so.
They go to witches.
Get their fortunes told.

WITCH WISDOM

Ever heard of the Magic 8 ball? Albert Carter created it. His mom was a psychic. She told fortunes. Albert made a toy to do the same thing.

Chapter 10

WITCHES TODAY

Witches live all around us.

There are active covens.

How do they meet?

Many meet online.

They talk to each other.

Ask for help.

Or advice.

MAGICAL POTIONS

There are many websites.

Message boards.

And social media groups.

Some witches blog.

They share recipes.

Show their hobbies.

Tell about their lives.

About how they became witches.

Some had a teacher.

Many were self-taught.

They studied.

Read books.

SPELL CASTING SET

Started a diary.
Planted a garden.

Most witches agree.
Being a witch is a choice.
It takes time.
And hard work.
But they found a way.

Witchcraft
A Modern Witch's Guide BLOG

ABOUT

RECIPES

TOOLS

GLOSSARY

altar: a raised place or table used for worship

blessing: support that helps you to do something

cauldron: a large metal pot

colonial: relating to the 13 first U.S. colonies

coven: a group of witches

crystal: a clear, hard mineral

curse: magical words that can harm

focus: to concentrate or pay attention

fortunes: a guess of the future

hex: magical words that can cause bad luck

karma: a person's actions have costs that cause good or bad things to happen to that person loyalty: committed to someone or something; faithfulness

mineral: a solid that is formed under the ground

newt: a small animal with wet skin and a lizard-shaped body; can breathe underwater and on land

pagan: a follower of a nature-worshipping religion; may believe in many gods

psychic: unique mental talent and power that cannot be explained

quartz: a hard, colorless mineral

reflective: capable of showing reflection, or image, on a surface

weave: move in a pattern; to twist or connect together

Wicca: a pagan religion based on the worship of nature

SEVEN WONDERS of the ANCIENT WORLD

Over 2,000 years ago
these places existed.
Or did they?
Some may be myths.
We know one is real.
It remains today.

Travelers talked about these places.
They called them wonders.
Seven in all.
Incredible sights to be seen.

The seven wonders are very old.
Ancient.
Most are no longer here.
They are part of the past.
How do we know about them?
From stories.
Ones told long ago.

Imagine.
A time with no TV.
No Internet. No phones.
People would talk. Tell stories.
Entertain. Inform.
Great storytellers drew crowds.
People listened.
They believed.

Chapter 5
TEMPLE OF ARTEMIS

The Greeks had many gods.
One was Artemis.
The goddess of the hunt.
People loved her.
They built her a shrine.
It was in Ephesus.

TEMPLE OF ARTEMIS

Date built: 550 BC
Location: Modern-day Turkey
How long to build: 120 years
What happened: Burned down

NONFICTION

9781680210293

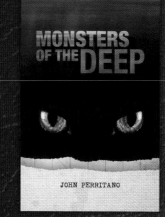

9781680210286

9781680210309

9781680210330